Factual Advisers
Dr. Lindsay Granshaw
Lecturer in the History of Medicine
The Wellcome Institute for the History of Medicine
London

Series Editor: Nicole Lagneau
Book Editor: Maria Ropek
Teacher Panel: Paula Bartley, Peter Hicks, Cathy Loxton
Designer: Ewing Paddock
Production: Rosemary Bishop
Picture Research: Donna Thynne

Printed and bound by Henri Proost, Turnhout, Belgium

Library of Congress Cataloging-in-Publication Data
Bryan, Jenny.
  Health and science / by Jenny Bryan.
    p. cm. — (Women history makers)
  Bibliography p.
  Includes index.
  Summary: Examines the participation of women in medical and scientific discoveries and in the growth of health care in France, Great Britain, and the United States through the lives of Marie Curie, Cicely Saunders, and Clara Barton.
  ISBN 0–531–19501–5
  1. Women in medicine — History — Juvenile literature. 2. Women in science — History — Juvenile literature. 3. Curie, Marie, 1867–1934 — Juvenile literature. 4. Barton, Clara, 1821–1912 — Juvenile literature. 5. Saunders, Cicely M., Dame — Juvenile literature. [1. Curie, Marie, 1867–1934. 2. Barton, Clara, 1821–1912. 3. Saunders, Cicely M., Dame. 4. Women in medicine. 5. Women in science.] I. Title. II. Series.
R692.B78 1988
610'.88042–dc19
[920]

Acknowledgements
We would like to thank Wayland (Publishers) Ltd for their kind permission to quote from *Joseph Lister* by A. J. Harding Rain; to Collins Publishers for permission to quote from *Marie Curie* by Robert Reid, 1974; to Century Hutchinson for permission to quote from *Joseph Lister and Antisepsis* by Kenneth Walker, 1956; to Heinemann Educational Books for permission to quote from *Madame Curie* by Eve Curie, 1937; to Edward Arnold for permission to quote from *Hospice: the Living Idea* edited by Dame Cecily Saunders *et al.*, 1981, and to Hodder & Stoughton for permission to quote from *Cicely Saunders* by Shirley du Boulay, 1984.

We acknowledge the source of quotes from the following: *Compact History of the US Red Cross* by Charles Hurd, Hawthorn Publishers, 1959; *The American Red Cross* by Patrick Gibo, Harper and Row, 1965. In addition we should like to thank those writers and publishers whom we have not been able to contact and whose work is reprinted in this publication. We invite them to contact us.

Photographs
The Publishers would like to thank the following for their permission to reproduce copyright photographs.
The American Red Cross; cover tl, cover back, 9l, 23b, 25, 26, 27 t&b, 28, 29 t&b, 30, 31.
Aspect Picture Library/Derek Bayes; cover b, 36r, 38b, 39, 43.
BBC Hulton Picture Library: cover r, 11l, 13b, 16 r&l, 17b, 21, 35.
BPCC/Aldus Archive: 10.
Barnaby's Picture Library: 24.
The Bridgeman Art Library: 15.
Cambridge Evening News; 34l.
Mary Evans Picture Library: 12.
Hackney Archives Department: 36l.
Hodder & Stoughton Ltd/Bryan Long: 9r, 38t.
Library of Congress, USA: 22.
The Mansell Collection Ltd,: 14b.
National Archives, USA: 23t.
Roger Viollet: 8, 14t, 18, 19 t&b.
Ann Ronan Picture Library: 11r, 13t, 17t.
Dame Cicely Saunders: 32, 34r, 37, 41.
Science Photo Library/Paul Shawbroom: 5.
Chris Taylor: 6–7.
Universal Pictorial Press Agency: 33t.
The Wellcome Institute Library/Punch: 33b.

Cover captions;
Top left: Clara Barton (1821–1912) and her team waiting to sail to Cuba, 1898 (see pages 30–31).
Bottom left: Cicely Saunders (b. 1918) (see pages 32–41).
Right: Marie Curie (1867–1934) (see pages 10–21).
Back cover: Calendar sheet, 1899 (see page 29)
Title page caption: testing for effects of a drug.

Jenny Bryan

Hampstead Press New York 1988

About this book

Half the people in the world are women. Yet women seldom appear in history books. One reason for this is that until recently, historians have mostly written about public events; in the past, many people thought that women should not take part in these. But, all the same, some women defied what people thought and worked to change society for the better. Their public achievements made history or would have, had historians remembered to take notice of them.

In the past, many historians have shared the traditional view that a woman's real place was at home, serving her family. If they found proof to the contrary, they didn't recognize it, or ignored it. (The only women they could never ignore were female rulers.) Often, too, they summed up women's achievements in a couple of sentences, or a footnote in small print. The books in this series aim to put the women history-makers back where they belong: in the world they helped to change, and in the way that we remember that world.

The three women you will read about here worked at different times, from the mid-19th to the late 20th centuries, and lived in different countries. The first, Marie Curie, was Polish but she lived most of her adult life in France; the second, Clara Barton, was American. The third, Cicely Saunders, is British. This book shows you what they have in common.

How to use this book
When studying the past, historians try to go back to what people of the past actually wrote and said. In the sections of the book marked "**Witness**," you can read some of the things said by people living at the time of Marie Curie and Clara Barton and who are living in Cicely Saunders' time today. You can also read comments from the women themselves.

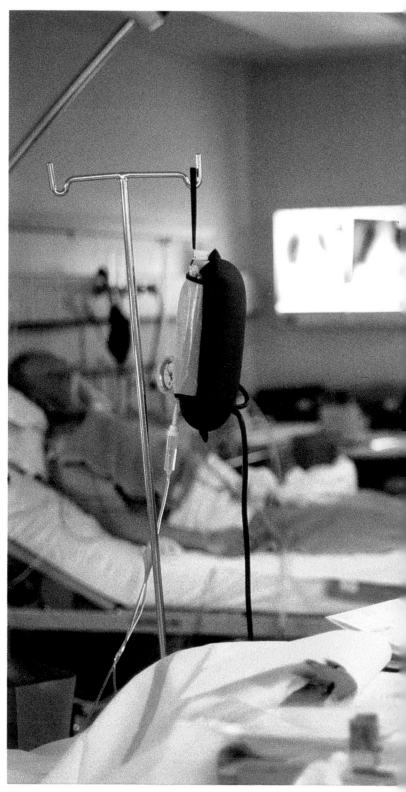

Scientific advances have enabled many people to live longer. Modern health services must try to mix high technology medicine with the traditional caring skills of medical staff, so that patients' quality of life is high, and anxiety and discomfort are minimized.

Contents

Women and history

Since ancient times, women have usually been the carers in society. Not only have they looked after the health of their own families but they have also nursed the sick, helped other women in childbirth and advised on the use of remedies, most of which were herbal before the 18th century, for all sorts of ailments. Nowadays, "old wives' tales" tend to be dismissed as nonsense but there is a lot of truth in many of the old medical sayings passed down through the generations.

Men have only come to dominate health care in the last two centuries. In the early 19th century, there was no formal medical training for doctors; instead, young men were apprenticed to experienced practitioners. Women were not allowed by their families to go and train in this way. Even when medical schools were set up later in the 19th century, women were rarely accepted though a few did train as missionary doctors. It was still considered unseemly for women to learn about the workings of the human body alongside men. In hospitals, the nurses were usually drawn from among the poor and it was only late in the 19th century that middle- and upper-class women started to train as nurses. They were always seen as handmaidens to the male doctors, carrying out their instructions. Working in a laboratory was unusual even for men and was not considered to be suitable women's work even by the most enlightened parents.

But there were some notable exceptions, women who ignored the stereotyped roles expected of them. Marie Curie was one of these. Both her parents were teachers and, unlike so many young women in the middle of the 19th century, she was encouraged to study. She chose to concentrate on physics. Her work on radioactivity has proved crucial to 20th-century medicine and science.

The two other women chosen for this book took on and developed the traditional caring role of women in society: Clara Barton set up the American Red Cross and Cicely Saunders pioneered the modern hospice movement for the care of the dying. They showed that it was possible for women to change public attitudes about the care of the sick.

In the rush to use new medical discoveries to enable people to live longer, the quality of life for patients was often forgotten. There was neither the time nor the hospital beds for those who could not be cured. The new scientific understanding of how the body worked

The importance of Marie Curie's (1867–1934) scientific discoveries was recognized with the award of two Nobel Prizes. Her research, pursued in the face of strong opposition, eventually won her the respect of scientists all over the world. Her work in the field of radioactivity has proved of enormous value in improving the way diseases are diagnosed and treated.

meant that many doctors saw their patients in terms of organs needing treatment, rather than as whole people with fears and emotions. This book charts some of the changes in attitudes towards health and science which have occurred during the past 100 years, and toward the women who brought about these changes. And it shows how three women in particular have influenced those attitudes.

Cicely Saunders (born in 1918) is the pioneer of the modern hospice movement. Thanks to her work, the incurably sick and the dying are given the same standard of medical care and attention as those who can be cured. Her message is being spread all over the world and thousands of cancer patients are now able to live with dignity, free of pain and fear.

Clara Barton (1821–1912) was the founder of the Red Cross in the United States. She single-mindedly begged, bullied and shamed the American government into signing the Geneva Convention and into setting up relief services to aid the needy in times of war and peace.

NEW ELEMENT

Radium

Blue light glimmered in the darkness from the tiny flasks lined up on shelves and tables in the old shed.

"Look! Look!" cried Marie Curie to her husband. "It's our radium." The material inside the flasks, like so many glow-worms, lit up Marie and Pierre's faces. For four years, they had stood over the huge tubs of raw pitchblende, a rock then used in the manufacture of glass. Marie and Pierre Curie had scooped the boiling liquid from the tubs in the yard as they belched foul smoke into the air. In the freezing shed, they had purified and re-purified the liquids. The work went on to produce a few grams of the element radium, which Marie Curie believed was held in the pitchblende.

Marie and Pierre Curie had first announced the discovery of radium to the Academy of Science in Paris on December 26, 1898. Marie Curie had measured very powerful rays, later to be called "radioactivity," which were produced by pitchblende, an ore of the element uranium. The pitchblende was certainly far more radioactive than uranium. Marie reasoned that there must be a new, undiscovered element in the pitchblende which produced the intense rays.

Her colleagues at the Academy were sceptical. They would not believe in the existence of the new element until they could see it for themselves, and it was weighed, measured and bottled. The whole idea of chemical elements which could emit powerful rays overturned many of the established laws of physics. The Parisian scientists were not prepared to revise their theories on the word of one Polish woman. Marie Curie was still an "unknown." But Pierre Curie was an established and respected physicist who had already made important contributions in the field of magnetism. Pierre Curie recognized the importance of his wife's work and, leaving his own, he joined her to prove the existence of radium. So the struggle began.

Marie Curie had begun her work on radioactivity in the wake of two of the most important discoveries of the latter part of the 19th century. In November 1895, a German physicist, Wilhelm Roentgen, saw how certain crystals could be made to produce an intense light, or fluorescence. He later found that he could use these fluorescent rays to photograph the bones in his wife's hand. Some of the rays passed straight through her hand and blackened a film. Others were absorbed by her bones so that the film remained white. The white sections formed an outline of her hand and finger

1904: the Curies shied away from the inevitable publicity which followed their discoveries. But their pictures were to be found in numerous magazines and newspapers of the day. The world wanted to know all about the "radium woman" and her husband.

Right, this was one of the first X-ray pictures ever taken, in 1896. It shows the left hand, complete with wedding ring, of the wife of Wilhelm Roentgen, the German physicist. He was the first to show that X-rays could be used to photograph the internal structures of the human body.

bones against the black background. This discovery has formed the basis of modern X-ray pictures.

Physicists throughout Europe were fascinated by Roentgen's pictures. Not only did they repeat the experiments, but they tried to find other elements which would produce similar rays. A French physicist, Henri Becquerel, was the first to demonstrate that uranium salts naturally produced a similar sort of fluorescence, even when kept in the dark.

It was this second discovery which triggered Marie Curie's interest. What were these rays? Why did certain elements, like uranium, produce the rays?

Marie set about a systematic analysis of all the elements she could think of. She begged and borrowed equipment, eked out her meager savings to pay for chemicals, and filled notebooks with her observations. All of this resulted in the bluish light years later, which brought with it the important discovery of radioactivity.

Above, Marie Curie's assistants stoke the fires which heat the pitchblende during the long separation process to produce pure radium.

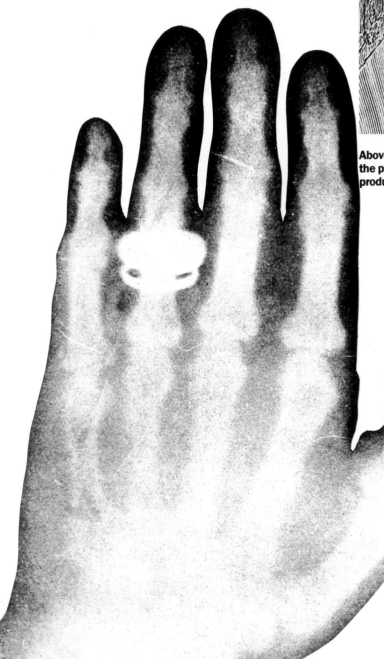

"*The great success of Professor and Madame Curie is the best illustration of the old proverb* coniuncta valent, *union is strength. This makes us look at God's word in an entirely new light: 'It is not good that the man should be alone; I will make him an help meet for him.'*"
Source: President of the Royal Swedish Academy of Sciences at the presentation of the Nobel Prize for Physics jointly to the Curies and Henri Becquerel, 1903. *Nobel Lectures 1901–1921,* 1967.

A new era

The 19th century was an exciting time for scientists. Not since the scientific revolution of the 17th century, when Sir Isaac Newton developed his laws of gravity, had there been such fervent activity.

Why was this period such a turning point for science and medicine? The answer lies in the changes in the way society was organized, which began in Britain a century before and quickly spread throughout Europe and America. After centuries of living off the land, people were moving to the towns, where there were more work opportunities, and where factories grew up in the late 18th and early 19th centuries. This was the start of urbanization, a process which helped push

society towards the high technology world of the 20th century. However, it also brought with it enormous health problems which challenged scientific and medical knowledge.

Thousands of people were crowded together in towns which had been built for much smaller numbers of inhabitants. Most roads were little more than muddy tracks and there were no drains or sewers. Household waste littered the streets because there were no organized disposal services, and fresh water supplies were often polluted.

With so many people living close together, infections spread like wildfire during the 18th and 19th centuries and epidemics engulfed whole cities. Families were wiped out by infectious diseases such as cholera and

Babies are placed in incubators, which are heated with stone hot-water bottles, at the Port-Royal Maternity Hospital in Paris in 1884. Better diet and vaccinations meant that fewer children died in infancy.

WITNESS

"Public health is the science and art of preventing disease, prolonging life and promoting mental and physical health . . . through organized community efforts for the sanitation of the environment, the control of communicable infections, the education of the individuals in personal hygiene, the organization of medical and nursing services for the early diagnosis and preventive treatment of disease . . . to ensure a standard of living adequate to the maintenance of health . . . as to enable every citizen to realize his birthright of health and longevity."
Source: A. Winslow, *The Evolution and Significance of the Modern Public Health Campaign*, 1923.

Left, until vaccines were developed, people relied on witchcraft and old wives' remedies to fight illness. Here, hundreds of French people dance round a bonfire outside the Palais de Justice in Marseilles in 1865, in the hope that they can banish the cholera epidemic.

Above, in addition to building drains and organizing rubbish disposal, some cities started fumigating public places in an attempt to rid them of germs. Here, passengers from Marseilles, which was badly hit by an outbreak of cholera in 1884, are being fumigated at Avignon station.

typhoid. Together with poor diet and poor living conditions, even more minor infections like colds and flu killed people. During the Industrial Revolution, people were often coming into contact with the organisms which caused these diseases for the first time, and they had no resistance against them.

On top of the epidemics, industrialization brought new diseases caused by the chemicals people worked with. These so-called "occupational diseases" were recognized as early as the first century AD, when slave mineworkers suffered mercury poisoning. But at the time of the Industrial Revolution, the diseases were seen on a huge scale: coalminers and metal grinders with lung diseases, chimneysweeps with genital cancers caused by soot ingrained in their skin, lead poisoning in factory workers, and pitch-and-tar handlers with skin cancers.

Major public health reforms to combat the effects of the Industrial Revolution started in Europe in the first half of the 19th century. These included the building of sewage systems and paving of roads, the setting up of safe water supplies and public education about the importance of hygiene. The reformers had theories about the causes of the diseases. They believed poisonous gases and liquids rose up from cesspits and rubbish dumps and attacked the population. The measures taken to improve public health proved effective. The doctors and scientists believed the ideas of the time, even if the explanations today would be quite different.

Discovery

Change in science comes slowly. Scientific break-throughs or exciting discoveries are followed by careful assessment and often criticism. Each new finding provides just one piece in the scientific jigsaw and it must be seen alongside the other pieces. How does it fit in with other discoveries? Does it confirm or conflict with earlier studies? Scientific theory evolves slowly in the light of a series of discoveries, and that is exactly what happened during the 19th century.

Urbanization and the diseases of industrialization were the trigger for the discoveries about infections and the organisms which cause them.

In 1796, a British physician, Edward Jenner, vaccinated a young boy against smallpox. He had noticed that milkmaids who caught a similar disease, cowpox, during the course of their work, were somehow protected against the much more deadly human disease, smallpox. He reasoned, correctly, that if he injected material from the scab of a woman with cowpox into the bloodstream of volunteers he could protect them against smallpox. His crucial experiment was in fact preceded by the work of Mary Wortley Montagu who introduced inoculation against smallpox to Britain after

Above, Pasteur developed his rabies vaccine in 1885. One group of Russians, who had been bitten by rabid wolves, walked hundreds of miles to Paris to be vaccinated.

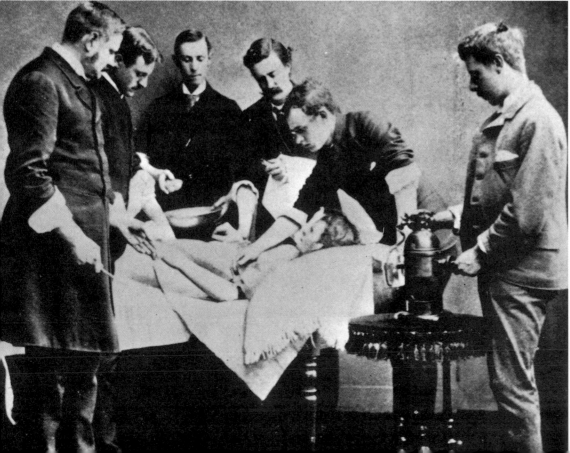

The use of carbolic spray in operating theaters to prevent wound infection, about 1870. The surgeons simply rolled up the sleeves of their outdoor clothes to perform surgery. With no protective gloves or masks, it was small wonder that so many patients caught infections from their doctors.

she had seen it practiced in Turkey in 1716–18. She used material from a smallpox scab but, because the disease was more serious than cowpox, the inoculation sometimes proved fatal.

The French scientist, Louis Pasteur, whose studies spanned 40 years in the middle of the 19th century, probably had the greatest impact on medical and surgical practise. His early work, showing that fermentation in wine, beer and milk was due to micro-organisms, inspired the British surgeon Joseph Lister to introduce the practise of antisepsis to operating theaters in 1865. Until the middle of the 19th century, infection, along with lack of general anesthesia, meant that widespread use of surgery was not possible. After a major amputation, of the leg, for example, around half of the patients died from infection, or sepsis.

Pasteur argued that micro-organisms, which could not be seen, were present in the air. They turned milk sour, and played a part in fermentation. Some micro-organisms caused disease, especially sepsis. Lister pointed out that it was open wounds which went septic. Seeing how sewage was disinfected, Lister argued that certain chemicals could kill the germs and that a chemical barrier should be placed between the air and the wound. He pioneered the use of diluted carbolic acid on surgical wounds and dressings with great success. Later, he started to insert tubes into wounds to drain away pus and thus further reduced the risk of fatal infection. Lister found it hard to convince his surgical colleagues and it was many years before antisepsis was routinely practiced and developed.

Robert Koch, the German microbiologist, argued that specific infections were caused by specific germs. Germs would be found in a patient which would produce the same disease if introduced into another person. Koch and others identified certain germs and medical scientists began to develop vaccines against them.

When, finally, the danger of infection was reduced, many more surgical operations were performed. This, too, brought its own problems. Surgeons became more and more daring, and patients could be treated almost like human guinea pigs. Often, they were left cruelly disfigured or seriously handicapped, victims of experimental medical techniques in the search for knowledge and the race for progress. Some people benefitted, but others were sacrificed.

WITNESS

Pasteur's work on micro-organisms was crucial to the search for the causes of infectious diseases, and for the development of vaccines against them.

Radioactivity

If doctors were slow to learn from the work of Pasteur and Lister, they were perhaps too quick to get on the radiation bandwagon set in motion by Wilhelm Roentgen, Henri Becquerel and Marie Curie. Many paid with their lives for their enthusiasm for the new radioactive chemicals before the dangers were recognized.

Marie Curie coined the term "radioactivity" to describe the rays which were continuously emitted by radium, uranium and related chemicals. It is now known that the atoms which make up these elements are unstable. Each atom is made up of a positively charged central core or nucleus which is "balanced" by the negatively charged electrons which surround it. If the balance is upset and the nucleus breaks down, energy is released in the form of rays and particles. These rays have different properties from the X-rays discovered by Roentgen and have since been called alpha and beta particles and gamma rays. It did not take long for doctors to realize that all these had the power both to destroy and to heal human tissue.

Marie Curie's hands were soon covered with small burns caused by radium. Even holding a sealed glass tube of the element could cause painful reddening of the skin which lasted for days. Henri Becquerel, who was following up the Curies' work, reported one day how his skin had burned through his clothes by a tube of radium he was carrying in his waistcoat pocket.

The scientists were unaware of the need for strict safety precautions when handling radioactive material. Even today, after scientists have seen the tragic consequences of radioactive fall-out following the atomic bombs in Hiroshima and Nagasaki (1945), there is still a lot that is not known about "safe" levels of radiation. The long-term effects of the 1986 Chernobyl disaster are yet to be seen. The scientists at the beginning of this century did not know about the dangers of radiation. It took decades to discover that radiation destroys the cells in tissues. It interferes with vital chemical reactions and damages the genetic material which holds all the information needed for the body to live and grow.

In the years after the discovery of radium, scientists were interested in understanding radium and were not thinking about the dangers of the new rays. One of the potential uses of radiation was to destroy cancerous growths. The first recorded cure came in Sweden in

Marie Curie joined dozens of other women and men who drove X-ray cars, nicknamed "Little Curies," around the battlefields of France during World War I.

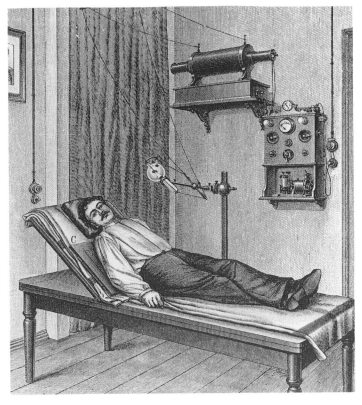

A drawing made in 1903 of an early X-ray machine taking pictures of a patient's chest. The X-rays are passed through his body from above and an image is formed on the photographic plate (C) behind his back.

Once scientists began to recognize the dangers of exposure to X-rays, they devised protective clothing. The outfit here was designed in 1909. Today, people who work in X-ray units sit behind protective screens and their exposure to X-rays is carefully monitored.

1899, when a form of nasal tumor was successfully treated. At first, the cancers treated tended to be on the skin but it was not long before machines were developed to send rays deep into the body. Much of the early work was trial and error. Often, doses were too high or too low or the radiation beam was inaccurate and destroyed healthy as well as diseased tissue.

Doctors of the day were divided; some favored X-ray sources while others used the radiation emitted by radium. The X-ray group were using their rays to diagnose as well as to treat illness. Roentgen's pictures of his wife's hands were just the beginning. Using doses of X-rays much lower than those to destroy tumors, scientists were producing pictures of organs deep inside the body. (Metals such as barium were consumed so that internal organs could be outlined.) With the onset of World War I, the new X-ray machines were in great demand for pinpointing the position of bullets in wounded soldiers. This saved many soldiers from painful exploratory operations and enabled surgeons to perform much smaller operations to remove the shrapnel.

Marie Curie recognized the need for such a service and drove through war-torn France in a mobile X-ray car. Eventually, she set up over 200 mobile and stationary X-ray rooms in cars and hospitals, and these were used to examine over one million men.

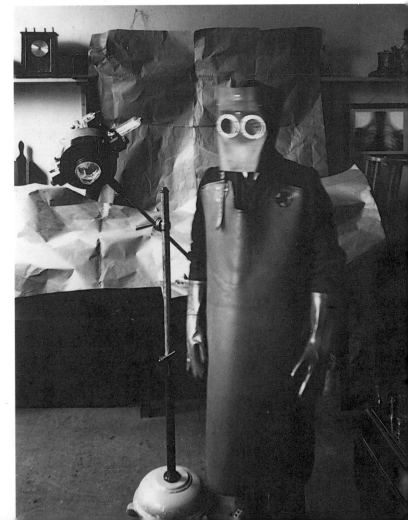

Pursuit of truth

There was never really any doubt in her mind. Marie Curie knew that she must publish the details of the methods she had painstakingly worked out to isolate radium from pitchblende during those four years.

"Physicists always publish their research work in full. If our discovery has a commercial future, that is an accident by which we must not profit. And radium is going to be of use in treating disease. . . . It seems to me impossible to take advantage of that," she said to Pierre Curie.

Only that morning, a letter had arrived from some American scientists asking for information about the radium work. Now that she had finally proved the existence of her element, it seemed that everyone wanted to use it. If she refused information and delayed publication about her discovery, Marie Curie could apply for a patent on the techniques she had used and her rights to her discovery would be protected. It would guarantee Marie Curie a percentage of the profits earned by anyone who used her techniques to manufacture and sell their products. The potential for radium was huge; Marie could be rich.

The scientific ideal was the dispassionate pursuit of truth, and the sharing of ideas with others. Many scientists, however, were often secretive about their results until they could publish and secure public recognition. But this was not Marie Curie's way. She had been poor from the moment she arrived in Paris in the autumn of 1891. She had left Poland, where she was born and brought up, with many regrets and assumed she would return after two or three years when she had completed her studies. She had spent six drab years as a governess in Poland and knew that, because of the Russian occupation of her country, there was little chance of any further education there.

Somehow, she completed two degree courses, in physics and then in math, at the Sorbonne in Paris. She lived in a cold attic room, with little money even for food, and all her time was spent in study. The determination which got her through her undergraduate years was to be crucial to her four-year struggle to prove that radium really existed.

By then, the pattern of her life was set. Any free time was spent with her family, and her greatest happiness outside the laboratory seems to have been the cycling holidays in northern France with her husband Pierre.

Marie Curie was one of the first women to play an important part in furthering scientific discovery. This was at a time when women were not encouraged to become interested in the sciences.

She had two daughters: Irene, who also became a physicist, and Eve, who was an accomplished singer. Details of their childhood achievements were often written alongside scientific references in Marie Curie's notebooks.

Marie Curie hated the publicity which went with her discovery of radium and later with the award of the two Nobel Prizes, one for Physics in 1903 and the second for Chemistry in 1911. She refused interviews and would return letters asking for autographs. In 1906,

WITNESS

"Marie Curie is, of all celebrated beings, the only one whom fame has not corrupted."
Source: Albert Einstein, quoted in article on Marie Curie by the Reverend C. A. Alington, Dean of Durham, *Daily Telegraph*, January 28, 1939.

"In science we must be interested in things, not persons."

"I am among those who think that science has great beauty. A scientist in his laboratory is a child placed before natural phenomena which impress him like a fairytale. Neither do I believe that the spirit of adventure runs any risk of disappearing in the world. If I see anything vital around me it is precisely that spirit of adventure which seems indestructible and is akin to curiosity."
Source: Marie Curie quoted in the same article.

"Christians will unite in doing honor to the young Polish girl who worked in her attic while the water froze in the jug and will share in her triumph on the great evening when she and her husband stood in the somber shadow and saw at last the particles of radium — their radium — shining like glow-worms in the dark."
Source: The Dean of Durham's article.

Marie and Pierre Curie were given bicycles as a wedding present and they spent many happy cycling holidays together. For a few weeks each year, they left their laboratories to explore the French countryside.

Right, Marie Curie's elder daughter, Irene, trained as a physicist and later joined the team in her Paris laboratory. She never had any doubts about her career and, like her mother, she combined family life with her work at the Radium Institute.

Pierre Currie died after falling under the wheels of a horsedrawn cart and Marie Curie became increasingly withdrawn. She continued her research in her laboratory in the newly-built Radium Institute in Paris, surrounded by a new generation of enthusiastic young physicists.

An American writer visiting Marie in her Paris laboratory discovered that in the whole of France there was less than a gram of radium and that its use was restricted to cancer treatment. Marie explained that above all, she would like a gram of radium of her own with which to continue her research. The cost of the radium in 1920 was $100,000, but a national campaign among American women called the "Marie Curie Radium Fund" raised the money. Marie repaid their generosity with an exhausting lecture tour of the United States in 1921.

Marie Curie's health was steadily deteriorating. The years of exposure to radioactive material were catching up with her. She died in 1934 from leukemia almost certainly caused by her radium.

MARIE CURIE

In the public eye

Even today, when the opportunities for women in science are greater, Marie Curie's contribution would have been outstanding. At a time when opportunities for women were very limited, it was even more remarkable.

Like any scientist, Marie Curie had to fight to get her ideas accepted. She was also greatly hampered by the appalling conditions in which she and her husband had to do their research. When the discovery of radium was finally recognized, the Curies were invited to many grand events. It was always Pierre who was invited to lecture about radium. Typical of such occasions was that at the Royal Institution in London, in 1903. Marie Curie was the first woman ever admitted through its doors. All of British science was gathered there, rows and rows of gentlemen scientists. Because she was a woman, Marie Curie had to sit silently while her husband spoke to the attentive audience.

In 1910–11, Marie Curie met with bitter opposition to her attempt to join the French Academy of Science. This was one of the greatest honors which could be bestowed on leading scientists of the day and many were determined that no women should be admitted. During the same period, she found herself at the center of a major public scandal concerning her friendship with another leading French scientist, Professor Paul Langevin. He was a married man and a series of letters between them found their way into the newspapers. Although Professor Langevin's wife certainly had something to do with the publication, there was evidence that French scientists were also involved. Subsequently, Marie Curie lost her fight to be elected

❝❝ WITNESS

"We salute in you a great scientist, a great hearted woman who has lived only through devotion to work and scientific abnegation, a patriot who, in war as in peace, has always done more than her duty. . . . You are the first woman of France to enter an academy but what other woman could have been so worthy?"

Source: M. Chauchard, President of the Academy of Medicine in France at the election of Marie Curie as a member, 1922. Quoted by Eve Curie, *Madame Curie*, 1938.

"We are joined by a deep affection which we ought not allow to be destroyed. Isn't the destruction of a

sincere and deep sentiment comparable to the death of a child which one has cherished and seen grow, and couldn't its destruction in certain cases be a greater misfortune than death. . . ."
Source: Letter from Marie Curie to Langevin. Quoted by Robert Reid, *Marie Curie*, 1974.

Despite the antipathy to her in France, Marie Curie was feted abroad wherever she went. Honorary degrees and titles were conferred on her by dozens of leading universities and scientific institutes. During her American tour in 1921, she met President Harding but the trip had to be cut short because of her ill health.

❞❞

to the French Academy of Science by a single vote.

Nearly 100 years later, the many memorials and charities in Marie Curie's name are a recognition of her achievements. She provided the knowledge for the development of many modern ways of finding and treating diseases. Also, her experiences, and those of her contemporaries, showed the importance of monitoring the long-term dangers as well as the benefits of any new discovery.

The equipment used by the pioneers of radioactivity in the early years of the 20th century now belongs in museums. But their machines were the forerunners of modern computerized machines which can process dozens of X-rays in seconds to create very detailed pictures of the inside of the body. Computers are also used in radiotherapy to direct the beams used to destroy tumors. This has greatly reduced the risk of damaging healthy tissues, but patients still suffer from the unwanted side effects of radiotherapy, such as tiredness, sickness and loss of appetite and weight.

Doctors remain far from satisfied with their current techniques. Frequent exposure to diagnostic X-rays does carry a small risk of causing cancer, and pregnant women cannot be X-rayed in case this damages their unborn babies. In the last 30 years, alternatives to X-ray diagnosis have been developed, such as ultrasound, which uses sound waves, and magnetic resonance imaging, which uses magnets and radio-waves to take pictures of the inside of the body. These techniques do seem to be free of unwanted effects, but to be sure, more testing and more evidence is needed and it will be many years before their safety can be established with certainty.

The practical applications of radium and all that has come since were far from Marie Curie's mind when she did her pioneering work with pitchblende. She, like most 19th- and 20th-century scientists, was more interested in discovery than practical application. Marie Curie searched for radium because it was there, and not for what it might do. In her world, the pursuit of science was everything; the benefit to medicine was a bonus.

BIOGRAPHY

1867 Born in Warsaw, Poland, Marie Sklodowska, the youngest of five children. Both parents are schoolteachers.
1891 Moves to Paris to study physics and then math at the Sorbonne University.
1895 Marries Pierre Curie, also a physicist.
1898 Announces the probable presence of a new radioactive element, called radium, in pitchblende.
1902 Finally isolates the elusive radium.
1903 Marie and Pierre Curie awarded Nobel Prize in Physics, jointly with Henri Becquerel, for their work on radioactivity.
1906 Death of Pierre Curie.

A few weeks later, Marie Curie begins lecturing at the Faculty of Science, University of Paris. This was the first time a woman had been appointed to a position in French higher education.
1911 Marie Curie awarded the Nobel Prize in Chemistry, the first person ever to be given two such awards.
1920–30 Travels throughout Europe and USA on lecture tours, while continuing her own research and teaching in Paris.
1932 Last visit to Poland for the opening of the Radium Institute in Warsaw.
1934 Dies at the age of 66.

Marie Curie, lecturing to leading scientists, shortly before her death. The exposure to radiation caused damage to her ability to make normal white blood cells which resulted in leukemia.

LESSONS OF WAR

On the battlefield

The booming of guns came from the valley below. No flash of uniform or glint of metal could be seen because the two armies were fighting in the woods. Three young soldiers lay where they had fallen, close together halfway down the hill. They had been easy targets for the bullets fired from below, and now the grassy hillside was littered with the bodies of the dead and dying.

A slight figure, followed by another and then another, moved carefully between the bodies. The women, their long skirts trailing in the grass, would stop and bend down over the bodies. They took out flasks and bandages from the bags slung over their shoulders. Sometimes, they did not stop but passed on quickly.

The three young men, one of them silent now, waited patiently for the figures in brown to make their slow way toward them. The guns were getting quieter and the groans of the wounded could be heard more clearly.

"Over here. Please, a drink of water," gasped one of the soldiers as the first woman came up. She bent down quickly and put a flask to the soldier's lips, looking carefully at the drying blood on his leg and checking for signs of other injuries.

"The bleeding's stopped. He'll live until we can get him to the field hospital," she thought. "After that, it's anyone's guess. If he's lucky he'll lose the leg, not his life."

The women moved on. This was the Battle of Cedar Mountain, which took place early in the American Civil War. It was at this time that the women's leader Clara Barton came to be known as the "Angel of the Battlefield" for her work with the wounded.

The American Civil War (1861–1865) was fought between the Northern states and the Southern "Confederacy," the states wanting to secede from the Union. One of the key arguments between the two sides was that of slavery. The South wanted to keep its slaves, while the North wanted them to be freed. Neither side was prepared for the horrors of war. It was nearly a hundred years since America had won its fight for independence. Since then, wars had been fought on foreign soil. So the soldiers and their families knew little of the horrific wounds, the pain and the suffering, and the epidemics of infection experienced in war.

Some lessons had been learned from the carnage of the Crimean War (1854–1856), when England, France and Sardinia fought Russia as the Czarist armies tried to establish a Mediterranean base in Turkey. There, Florence Nightingale and her team of nurses had shown the need for basic field hygiene and sanitation,

Women of the Sanitary Commission in action in the USA in 1864. The Commission was set up to investigate army living conditions, with a view to prevention of disease, and to find out how private funding could supplement government money. It was created because American women wanted to be of real help during the Civil War.

"I thought that night if heaven ever sent out a holy angel, she must be one, her assistance was so timely."
Source: Brigade Surgeon James L. Dunn, at the Battle of Cedar Mountain, speaking of Clara Barton. Quoted by Charles Hurd *Compact History of the American Red Cross*, 1959.

"More than once she saved her skin on the battlefield by a last-minute dash on horseback when she had stayed to tend the wounded until the Confederates were close at hand."
Source: an observer quoted in same book as above.

Above, a group of wounded Union soldiers, 1863. Chief of Nurses for the Union Army was Dorothea Dix, who mobilized thousands of women and, like Clara Barton, followed the battles.

Right, three nurses from the Civil War, wearing nurses' hats that must have been difficult to keep clean on the muddy battlefields.

adequate rations and proper nursing. Four months after the nurses started work in Scutari near Constantinople in 1855 the death rate among soldiers admitted to the hospital had fallen from 42 per cent to 2 per cent. At the same time, the Jamaican-born nurse Mary Seacole was taking her medical bag into the thick of battles in the Crimea. She was admired for her medical expertise, and many soldiers owed their lives to her.

But how were the soldiers fighting in the American Civil War to be spared the fate of those who had fought the Crimea six years earlier? There was no organized health care in the US at that time. A few hospitals had been set up in the larger cities, but these were often hundreds of miles from the battlefields and the wounded stood little chance of reaching them alive.

On to this chaotic scene came Clara Barton and the other women she rallied to the cause. They drove their wagons of food, clothing and medical supplies to the battlefields and set up field hospitals to care for the sick and kitchens to feed the soldiers. Gradually, women all over the country, from all social classes, grouped together to bring help to the armies. This was the start of the women's emergency relief organizations, which were to continue working long after the guns of the Civil War fell silent.

The Red Cross

While the women of America were organizing relief groups to help the wounded of the Civil War, European leaders were meeting in Switzerland to discuss how to improve the treatment of soldiers wounded in battle. On August 22, 1864, they drew up and agreed to a set of rules in the form of the Geneva Convention. This specified how the injured should be treated humanely in times of war. But it was to be nearly 20 years before the US signed the agreement.

The first National Relief Organizations were set up in Europe in 1863. Their aim was to organize field hospitals and evacuation routes quickly and efficiently in time of war. They became known as the Red Cross after the emblem was chosen at the signing of the Geneva Convention to distinguish medical workers from troops on the battlefields. Red Cross workers and equipment were to be protected from attack because they took no sides and carried no weapons. Even in the fiercest wars, this tradition has rarely been broken. The red cross on a white background is the reverse of the Swiss flag, under which the Geneva Convention was signed.

One by one, national governments learned the lessons of war. Better weaponry was causing more casualties, and so the need for proper nursing facilities for the wounded became apparent, as well as the need for healthy recruits. A lifetime of poor diet and bad living conditions showed up in the undersized, infected bodies of the soldiers dropped into the armies of Europe and America. It was impossible to convert them into the tough fighting machines demanded by modern warfare and thousands died before they reached the battlefields. Army leaders urged improvements in public health care.

Progress was slow after the Civil War. However, with the growth of towns and of the middle classes, who increasingly found they needed care in institutions rather than at home, more hospitals were built. Water supplies and sewage systems were improved as urbanization grew. The discoveries of Pasteur and Lister were applied in operating theaters to help reduce infection.

By the time the United States counted its casualties in World War I (1914–1918), it was found that for the first time the number of deaths from disease was smaller than those in battle.

It was during World War I that the first large-scale use of tetanus vaccine dramatically reduced the toll from wound infection, and antibacterial fluids (or

The varied duties of members of the Sanitary Commission depicted in an 1864 picture. They range from nursing the sick and dying to holding "bring-and-buy" sales to raise money for supplies for the army. The government relied heavily on American women to raise money for medical supplies, food and clothing for the soldiers.

The GREATEST MOTHER in the WORLD

 **WITNESS**

"I had learned the use of the Red Cross, had learned to love and respect it — to realize what misery and what lives it would have saved in our Civil War if we had had it, and day by day, I pledged myself anew to its service in my own country if I could ever see it introduced there, and I promised the societies and sovereigns of other nations to use every endeavor to bring it to the knowledge and the attention of the American government and of the American people."
Source: Clara Barton, while serving as a volunteer relief worker during the Franco–Prussian War, 1870–1871. Quoted by Patrick Gilbo, *The American Red Cross*, 1965.

"antiseptics") were widely adopted for use against infection in makeshift operating rooms. Intravenous fluids were used for the first time to replace blood lost in surgery, which was a common cause of surgical shock. Blood transfusion was still in its infancy, following the discovery of the major blood groups in 1901.

At last, either with vaccination or antisepsis, army doctors were able to prevent some of the infections which had killed so many soldiers previously. But there was still no effective way of treating infections once they had started. The search for an "internal antiseptic" had been going on since before World War I. In the mid-1930s, the sulphonamides were developed, and so doctors had the predecessors of modern antibiotics at their disposal.

Production of penicillin was rushed ahead during the early years of World War II. However, there was not enough to go around. The demand was too great. Doctors had to choose, for example, between giving it to soldiers with venereal diseases thus enabling them to go straight back into the fighting, and giving it to the wounded who might take much longer to get well enough for battle, if at all.

Ironically, many of the medical advances which we now take for granted were made during the 19th and early 20th century because of war. Governments anxious to keep their armies strong and healthy encouraged research that developed life-saving drugs and medical techniques for soldiers, but which were later used for everyone.

Natural disasters

Red flames leapt against the skyline as far as the eye could see and the air was filled with choking smoke as forest fires swept across the state of Michigan in September 1881. Families watched in horror as their homes burned to the ground. Whole towns had to be evacuated and many people died in the flames.

Clara Barton and her growing army of women volunteers went into the inferno. They had learned a lot since the Battle of Cedar Mountain, and they were better organized to distribute the food, clothing, blankets and medical supplies which they brought with them. Clara Barton had traveled to Europe after the Civil War and seen how the new relief agencies were establishing themselves. She wanted America to have its own Red Cross and she knew that success in Michigan could sway the senators she had been lobbying in Washington.

Memories of the fight for independence from Britain (1776–1783) left successive US governments wary of any agreements with Europe, and they had not signed the Geneva Convention. Clara Barton hoped for an ally in the new president inaugurated in 1880. But within a year, President Garfield was assassinated. So, the lobbying began again.

The American National Red Cross was set up by Clara Barton and her followers on May 21, 1881. However, without the support of the US Congress, it could never have the power and influence it needed to be effective. Six months after the Michigan fires, Clara Barton got her way. Congress approved the treaty covering the Red Cross as it was originally set up in Europe and in July 1882, the United States signed the Geneva Convention.

"So it was done. . . . I had waited so long and got so weak and broken I could not even feel glad," commented Clara Barton.

The work of the relief organization she had started was changing. During the Michigan fires, the emphasis

Orphans from the Cherry Mine disaster in 1909. The Red Cross set up a fund for widows and orphans.

Workers sort seed potatoes ready for planting after widespread crop damage during the South Carolina hurricane of 1893. The American Red Cross started an aid program which fed over 30,000 homeless and starving people.

was as much on helping the survivors as it was on emergency help. Families needed new homes and their belongings had to be replaced. Often, the wage earners needed new jobs and this could mean learning new skills, especially if they had suffered permanent injuries in the fires. The teams of volunteers found that their work was not over when the fires went out. Yet their help was also soon needed elsewhere.

In 1884, the Mississippi river burst its banks in Ohio. The flood was a very different type of disaster from Michigan but the results were similar. Seven thousand families were made homeless and hundreds left without a livelihood when the floodwaters went down. Overcrowding of the survivors and lack of sanitation made a perfect breeding ground for infections like cholera and typhoid. The resources of the American National Red Cross were stretched to breaking point.

These first two major disasters, with the floods in Johnstown (1889) and the hurricane on Sean Island (1893) brought home the need for many more local relief groups. Some people did not like "do-gooders" from another state descending on them in times of trouble. Clara Barton and her followers were thrown out of Florida when they tried to help there in a yellow fever epidemic.

The early days of the American Red Cross showed women in America how effective they could be. There were many things to be done, from helping the homeless to raising money for hospitals and schools. Volunteer groups sprang up all over the country and women from all social classes became involved.

 WITNESS

"There is no doubt that the day is not far distant — if it has not already come — when the American people will recognize the Red Cross as one of the wisest and best systems of philanthropic work in modern times."
Source: Editorial in the *Chicago Inter Ocean*, following the Ohio–Mississippi floods, 1884.

Clara Barton's Red Cross first saw relief action in 1881, when it organized help for the hungry and homeless following the massive forest fires which swept the state of Michigan. This drawing, called "Help or I perish," was published in *Leslies' Weekly*. It shows the women of the relief organizations going to the aid of those in need.

Campaign

Clara Barton could hardly believe what she was seeing, but there it was in black and white: the name of nearly every country she could think of included in the Geneva Convention, except the USA. She was so ashamed. She had come to Switzerland at the invitation of a Swiss youth she had nursed in one of the last battles of the Civil War. He had told her about the newly formed Red Cross and she wanted to see it for herself.

Lecture tours across the States after the war had brought her considerable wealth and recognition and now she was able to travel and dress in style. She had met other influential women of the time, such as the writer Louisa May Alcott, who had been a nurse during the Civil War, and Susan B. Anthony, who tried to interest her in the equal rights movement which was just starting after the Civil War. It was a time when women were becoming more active in many areas, including equal rights, and some women decided suffrage for women should be demanded. But Clara Barton was already committed to her relief work.

Arriving in Geneva in 1869, she had been delighted to find that her fame had gone before her and many people knew of her exploits on the US battlefields. Her smiles had quickly disappeared, however, when she realized how advanced the European agencies were compared to her own organization in the USA.

"We must have a Red Cross too and I shall make it happen," she said to herself.

From Geneva, Clara Barton traveled through France and Germany and supervised the distribution of supplies in the Franco–Prussian War, when France was fighting the German states. In 1871, Clara Barton moved her headquarters to Paris and launched her own relief program for the soldiers.

Two years later, Clara Barton returned to the USA, plagued by poor health and failing eyesight. But she was already planning her campaign for an American Red Cross. She hoped that her earlier political contacts in Washington would prove useful.

Before the Civil War, Clara Barton had left her teaching job and started work in 1854 in the Patent Office in the capital, where people registered their new inventions. She worked hard and quickly moved up the scale but her success did not last long. Her boss changed in 1857, and her new employer did not believe in men

Above, Clara Barton, at the height of her power and fame. She encouraged women to be active in the organization of relief services, to help both the wounded in war and the victims of natural disasters such as fire, flood and famine. "Everybody's business is nobody's business, and nobody's business is my business," she once said.

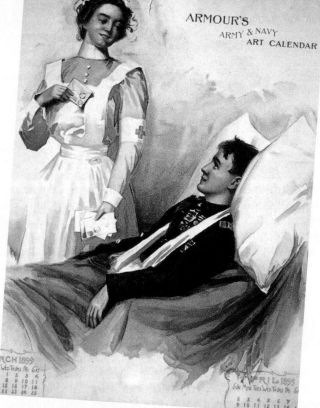

Romanticized calendar sheet for 1899, showing a nurse and soldier during the Spanish–American War. The reality was very different, with the poorly trained and equipped medical services trying to help the sick and wounded in makeshift hospitals and muddy camps.

and women working together in government offices. Clara Barton was dismissed but the Patent Office was very busy, and she continued working for it at home. In 1860, when her old enemy left, she was invited back.

This time, she was determined to make important friends who could protect her from any future attacks. One of these was Senator Henry Wilson. He was so impressed with her hard work and efficiency that he recommended her for a more important job in the offices of the postmaster general.

So, it was to her Washington contacts that she went ten years later, when she returned from Europe. She needed powerful allies to help her establish the American Red Cross, and it was her success in Michigan that finally convinced them.

" WITNESS

THE CHALLENGE
A CARTOON APPEARING IN THE PHILADELPHIA "LEDGER," LAST NOVEMBER.

"Ladylike, sympathetic, energetic and marvellously forceful . . . still patient, still persistent, rising at 4 or 5 o'clock in the morning and working until late at night, living with such simplicity of life that no soldier ever lived upon a smaller ration or slept upon a narrower or simpler bed than that upon which she slept night after night, always with a light at the head of the bed where she might, as thoughts came to her in the night, write down those thoughts."
Source: Dr. William E. Barton, cousin and biographer to Clara Barton. Quoted by Charles Hurd, *Compact History of the American Red Cross*, 1959.

Left, a 1909 cartoon depicts the battle which the American Red Cross waged against tuberculosis. It would be another 50 years before TB was effectively wiped out.

"Miss Barton had an astonishing imagination that any experienced army officer would recognize in reading the quotations from her diary and other papers in her biography."
Source: Mabel Boardman, Clara Barton's successor at the American Red Cross, in 1940 when Clara Barton was nominated, unsuccessfully, for the Hall of Fame of Great Americans. Quoted by Patrick Gilbo, *The American Red Cross*, 1965.

"The Red Cross has settled itself. I will resign even my membership and when I can get out of my house and hand all that belongs to the new organizations, it will be the same as if I had never known it."
Source: Clara Barton diaries, 1904, quoted in same book as above.

Medicine's "failures"

Cicely Saunders left the ward quietly, a smile on her face. She and David Tasma had been laughing all afternoon but now he had dropped off to sleep. They both knew David had little time left, and they wanted to talk about so many things. They had met when he came into hospital, dying from cancer.

An idea was forming in Cicely Saunders' mind. There were so many people like David, dying alone and in pain, or in very busy wards. They deserved help, both for their physical and their emotional sufferings. How could she bring them that help? She wondered if she could convince people to give their money and their support in order to build a place where the dying could be cared for properly. It would be a place where there would be no pain, only peace and dignity.

When he died, David Tasma left £500 towards that first building. "I'll be a window in your home," he said. That was in 1948, and it was nearly 20 years before the window was in place and the home open. Why did it take so long? The answer lies in the way medical science changed in the first half of the 20th century and in how doctors and nurses saw their role in the care of the sick.

The improvements in hygiene and living conditions which had begun in the 19th century continued. Powerful new drugs and more skilled and daring surgical operations were developed. More people were living to old age than ever before and far fewer children died in infancy than at the turn of the century. In Britain in 1948, the National Health Service (NHS) was set up so that everyone in the United Kingdom could go to their doctor or be treated in a hospital, free of charge and benefit from the new discoveries in medicine.

Expectations were high. Doctors were able to cure people with diseases such as tuberculosis and diphtheria. Families who, only a generation before, had seen brothers, sisters and children die of such infections in their youth now marveled at the benefits of modern medicine.

The medical profession soon found itself with a lot to live up to. It was hard to cope with their failures, the patients they could not cure. The demands on the fledgling NHS were great and there was no provision for institutional care for the dying. There were a few homes with limited beds in London for the dying, but the great majority of those who could not be treated were sent home, to be cared for by their families as best they could. However, the family network was also changing. Women were the traditional carers of sick members of the family. But, as more women went out to work, there was no one at home to care for the elderly and the infirm. Smaller families meant that there were fewer grown-up children to share the burden of caring for a sick or dying relative.

When the burden became too great, sick relatives were admitted to hospital wards where, at least, they could be kept clean and fed. Often, they lived out their last weeks in a frightened and painful world. Until, that is, Cicely Saunders decided that improvements in the care of the dying were long overdue. She had to convince both the medical profession and the public that it was just as important to care for the dying and to learn more about pain as it was to find cures for the sick.

While working as a medical social worker, Cicely Saunders met David Tasma. From their discussions came the idea for St. Christopher's Hospice.

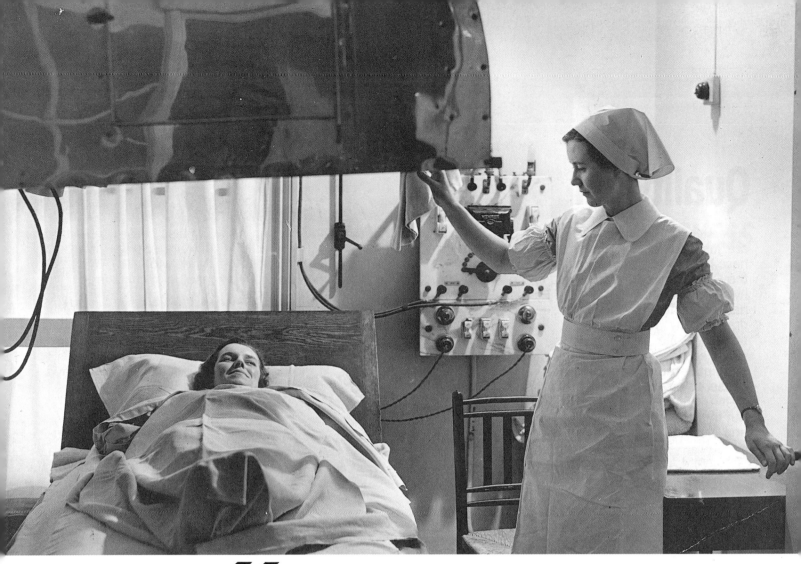

Deep heat treatment was used above to relieve pain. All too often, patients were told little about the frightening looking equipment which was used to treat them and many suffered needless fears and anxieties because of the lack of information.

Right, accident patient (suddenly reviving, to doctor who had pronounced life to be extinct): "I ain't dead, Guvnor." Attendant: "Now, then, lie down. The doctor knows." The idea that "doctor knows best" meant that until the 1960s and 1970s many cancer patients were not given adequate painkillers. Doctors were slow to accept new ideas in pain control, and patients were unwilling to question their authority.

"WITNESS

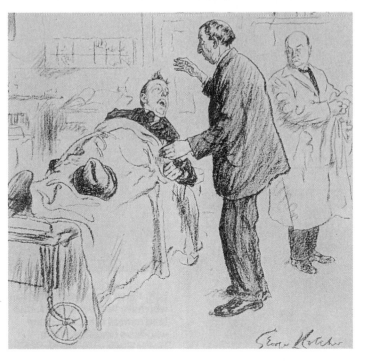

"It used to be just like a vice gripping my spine . . . I didn't get my injections regularly — they used to leave me as long as they could and if I asked for them sometimes they used to say, 'No, wait a bit longer.' They didn't want me to rely on the drugs that were there, you see. They used to try and see how long I could go without an injection. . . . I used to be pouring with sweat, you know, because of the pain. . . . I couldn't speak to anyone, I was in such pain."
Source: New patient talking to Cicely Saunders at St. Joseph's Hospice about her previous treatment, London, tape recording, about 1963.

Care of the dying

The word "hospice" goes back many centuries and originally meant "a house of rest and entertainment for pilgrims, travelers or strangers." It is only since the middle of the last century that it has taken on its modern meaning, that of a home for the care of the dying. Today, nine out of ten beds in British hospices are reserved for people with cancer. Some are about to die; many are admitted for treatment of physical symptoms and others to give their families a break from caring for them. All hospices are also ready to offer people some form of spiritual help, whatever their religious faith, though it is never forced on anyone. The intention is to help those trying to cope with the fact that they may soon die.

Patients who know they will die soon experience a wide range of emotions, including anger, guilt, fear and regret, and most are glad of the chance to talk through these feelings with someone who is willing to listen and understand. Often, family and friends are the hardest ones to talk to and experienced hospice staff can help fill the gap. About 140,000 people die of cancer each year in Britian. Of these, probably 40,000 have been in touch with a hospice, either as an in-patient or at home, where they are visited by hospice nurses. The hospice approach has greatly influenced

St. Joseph's Hospice was founded in 1905 to care for the chronically sick and the dying. The original building has now been replaced by an up-to-date complex. There is also a Home-Care Service operating from the hospice, which provides help for the dying in their own homes.

The Little Flower Ward.
St. Joseph's Hospice. Mare Street, Hackney. E.8.

Above, hospice patients are encouraged to get out and about as much as possible. A visit to the local pub was a regular event for Sam, a resident of St. Christopher's in 1983. Volunteers are always on hand to drive patients wherever they wish to go.

Children of patients and staff play together at St. Christopher's nursery. Family therapy is an important part of care and it is often the children who find it hardest to express their feelings when parents are very ill. A sympathetic ear from trained counselors can help relieve fears and anxieties.

WITNESS

"The biggest difference is, of course, this feeling of calm. I don't get worked up, I don't get upset, I don't cry, I don't get very, very depressed — you know. Really gloomy thoughts were going through my mind, and no matter how kind people were, and people were ever so kind, nothing could console me, you see. But since I've been here, I feel more hopeful as well."

Source: Same patient as on page 33, speaking to Cicely Saunders after a short time at St. Joseph's Hospice. Quoted by Shirley du Boulay, *Cicely Saunders*, 1984.

the care of the dying. Even cancer patients who spend their last days or weeks in hospital benefit from the ideals behind the modern hospice movement.

Early attempts at hospice care in the late 19th and early 20th century centred on dedicated care by nuns and nurses. In London, St. Joseph's Hospice was set up in 1905, the Marie Curie Memorial Foundation (formed in honor of the famous Polish physicist) opened its first home for people with cancer in 1952, and there was a small number of other homes. Patients were kept as comfortable as possible but there were few drugs to relieve their pain, which can be very great. The start of effective pain control for people with cancer has been traced back to around 1935 at St. Luke's Hospital, London. A far-sighted nurse started to give morphine-based drugs regularly by mouth to relieve pain, but it was to be another 30—40 years before this approach was widely adopted.

About two thirds of people with advanced cancer suffer some pain. The painkilling properties of the morphine-like drugs have been known for centuries both to physicians and to addicts who use heroin and similar drugs to get "high." But doctors and nurses treating

cancer pain were reluctant to use these drugs because they feared that patients would become addicted, need larger and larger doses and live in a drug-induced haze. What they ignored was that cancer patients react to morphine very differently than healthy people.

It was during the 1950s and 1960s, while working at St. Joseph's Hospice, that Cicely Saunders and others demonstrated the importance of giving morphine and other painkilling drugs regularly every few hours, and not waiting until the pain came back. They showed that relieving the fears and anxieties of many cancer patients, with drugs or emotional help, could reduce the pain, too. And they found that careful nursing could get rid of many other physical problems. These include constipation caused by morphine, weight loss resulting from poor appetite, and bed sores as a consequence of lying or sitting down for long periods.

It has taken time for news of the hospice methods to spread. Even today, some medical staff fail to give cancer patients effective pain relief. But those working in hospices know how important it is to treat both the physical and emotional problems of cancer patients, so that they can live with dignity and in comfort.

Patients' needs

"I think if I had been happier when I was young, I would have got married and settled down and then I would never have started the hospice movement. It was because I always felt undervalued that I felt at one with other undervalued people, and I became determined to help them." (Cicely Saunders, 1987)

Nicknamed "cock-a-rooster" by her father, after a gawky bird with a long neck and big feet, Cicely Saunders was painfully shy as a child. At school, she never found it easy to make friends. At home, she was aware from an early age of the unhappiness between her parents. Her father was a dynamic man, while her mother would spend days in her room and found it hard to cope with her three chidlren.

As a baby, Cicely was often cared for by nannies, and later she was packed off to boarding school. It was only in the last years at school that she began to show some of the talent which set her on the road to no less than three training courses: nursing, medical social work, and, finally, medicine. She qualified as a doctor when she was nearly 39. Her conversion to Christianity in 1945 was an important milestone in pointing her towards her future work. Cicely Saunders decided that if she was to change doctors' attitudes to the care of the dying, she had to do so from inside the profession,

Cicely Saunders has said that she is never going to retire. She is determined that the hospice ideals which she initiated will be carried on by future generations of doctors and nurses all over the world.

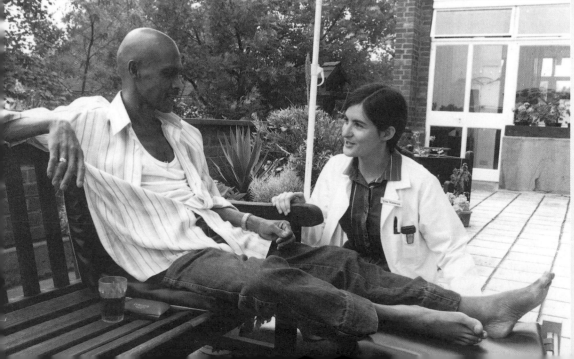

St. Christopher's is also a training ground for young doctors and nurses who see their future with the care of the dying. Regular courses on all aspects of cancer care are held at the hospice, and trainees learn about the importance of being able to communicate with their patients.

as one of them. She started the campaign for her own hospice while she was working with the nuns at St. Joseph's Hospice in London. Cicely Saunders brought her new expertise in pain control, originally learned at St. Luke's Hospital where she had been a volunteer evening nurse, and combined it with the loving care and spiritual support which were a feature of St. Joseph's. It was the combination of these two approaches which were to form the basis for the modern hospice movement, which started the day Cicely Saunders finally opened the doors of St. Christopher's Hospice in southeast London, on July 24, 1967. The hospice was dedicated not only to care but also to research and teaching in the control of distress.

In 1959, she had estimated that she would need £200,000 to build and furnish the home but this was soon revised upwards. Where was all the money to come from?

Cicely Saunders quickly got a few important politicians on her side. She felt that St. Christopher's should be run independently from the NHS, but she knew that she would need the backing of the Regional Hospital Boards in providing grants. She was successful in this. Charities became interested as Cicely met their representatives and sometimes showed them around St. Joseph's. Other grant-giving bodies, such as the City Parochial Foundation, the Drapers' Trust, the Nuffield Foundation and the King Edward's Hospital Fund, also fell under her spell. Numerous public appeals saw the campaign edge towards its target, and then came the great day on March 22, 1965 when the first soil for the new building was dug.

In 1963, while St. Christopher's was still at the planning stage, Cicely Saunders met a Polish artist, Marian Bohusz-Szyszko. Their courtship was unorthodox, with neither of them apparently knowing what they wanted. It was not until 1980, after they had been together for 17 years, that they married, almost in secret: Marian for fear that his Polish friends would think he had married for money, Cicely because she did not want to be in the newspaper headlines. Many of Marian's paintings now hang in the hospice, helping to make it more home-like.

Over 10,000 patients and their families have now passed through St. Christopher's Hospice. It has 78 beds and numerous day rooms where patients, families and friends can sit and chat. The NHS pays less than half of the total cost of care, and the rest is paid for by gifts and grants.

St. Christopher's was the first research and teaching hospice, and it set out to lay the scientific foundations of terminal care. Cicely Saunders strongly believed that patients should be able to live as fully as possible till they died, with good pain control, they should be able to choose where they were to die, and also that the patients' families should be given appropriate help and support. Everything should suit the caring of the dying, and the hospice building was designed around the needs of the patients, for it is their place.

Cicely Saunders is now Chair of the Council of Management at St. Christopher's, and she regularly takes her turn at medical duty on weekends. At the top of the building is her husband's studio, and below is Cicely Saunders' office, where she is to be found each day.

There is always time for a chat at St. Christopher's. Ward rounds are informal, and patients are encouraged to talk about their illness and anything which is bothering them.

WITNESS

"Cicely came to see me in the Ministry of Health . . . I thought, 'This woman's mad.' I, who am a civil servant, had kittens about the way she approached the questions of budgets, but her vision was both detailed and practical. She is a visionary."
Source: Dame Albertine Winner, 1961, now President of St. Christopher's Hospice. Quoted by Shirley du Boulay, *Cicely Saunders*, 1984.

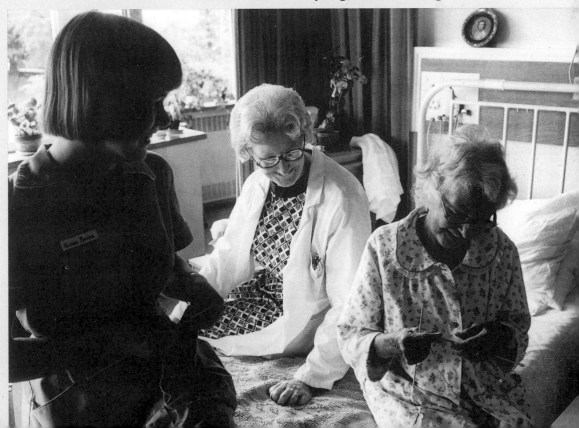

In the public eye

In 1980, the woman who as a child had been too shy even to get on the train to school was given the title "Dame" Cicely Saunders. She proudly displays the honor alongside other framed awards she has received for her work as founder of the modern hospice movement.

Her work has not been limited to the 78-bed home in southwest London. Cicely Saunders has written widely about the approach of hospice care and has lectured all over the world. In 1963, Cicely Saunders traveled to the United States where she discussed care of the dying with doctors, nurses, hospital chaplains, psychiatrists and social workers. She learned from the experience but she also inspired and brought together people from Canada and the United States who were interested in caring for the dying, and she greatly influenced the development of the hospice movement there. Today, hundreds of hospices exist all over the world.

The philosophy behind the movement has been applied in many countries in different ways. For example, in the USA, the emphasis is more on non-medical volunteers visiting cancer patients at home. In Britain, there are now over 100 hospice-style units and many more teams who visit cancer patients in their homes, offering the special combination of pain control, family support, and spiritual help, which was pioneered at St. Christopher's.

But Cicely Saunders' achievements were not just in bricks and mortar or even in a philosophy for the care of the dying. She started a greater openness towards patients with incurable diseases, urging doctors and nurses to talk to their patients and to answer their questions honestly and humanely. There is no doubt that, slowly, the medical profession is getting better at communicating with patients, and learning that silence brings only fear and uncertainty. Recently another doctor, Vicky Clement-Jones, started a cancer information service called BACUP (British Association of Cancer United Patients) when she discovered, as a cancer patient, how hard it still is to get advice.

So where does the hospice movement go from here? Cicely Saunders is determined to leave plenty of highly trained medical staff to continue the work she has begun. She believes that care of the chronically sick and the dying needs special skills; it should not simply be swallowed up by the general health care system but can be introduced, sometimes by specially trained teams, into general hospitals. This means that there needs to be a proper career structure for doctors and nurses who decide to specialize in the care of the dying. There also needs to be careful planning for future hospices, to ensure that they maintain the high standards of nursing care which have already been set.

Cicely Saunders would also like to see the ideals of the hospice movement applied to other areas of medicine, such as the care of the mentally ill. She believes that the very different nursing requirements of the mentally ill or those with other incurable diseases, such as AIDS, means that they will need their own hospices. But attitudes towards the incurably ill need to change within the community as well as in the medical profession. Cicely Saunders started the ball rolling but we too must help keep up the momentum.

Left, in 1977, Cicely Saunders received the Lambeth Doctorate from the Archbishop of Canterbury for her work with the dying, one of many awards she has received in recognition of her pioneering work.

WITNESS

BIOGRAPHY

"We do not consider that there would be any advantage in promoting a large increase in the number of hospices at present and we recommend the way forward is to encourage the dissemination of the principles of terminal care through the health service and to develop an integrated system of care with emphasis on coordination between the primary care sector, the hospital sector, and the hospice movement."
Source: *Report on Terminal Care*, 1980. British Department of Health and Social Security (DHSS)

"Like all good movements the impact of the hospice movement does not depend on bricks and mortar but on the interest its ideas generate and the changes in practical care which these have brought about."
Source: G. Young in *Hospice: The Living Idea*, 1981, edited by Dame Cicely Saunders, D. and H. Summers and N. Teller.

"Your work with those who face death has become an inspiration to patients and their families. You have combined the learning of science and the insight of religion to relieve physical pain and mental anguish, and have advanced the awareness of the humanistic aspects of patient care in all states of illness. First as a nurse, then as a social worker, you saw the special need of the dying patient, and as a physician you founded St. Christopher's Hospice. To it have come doctors, nurses, social workers, and clergy from nations around the world to work and study with you. Yale University, in admiration of your contribution to science and humanity, confers upon you the degree of Doctor of Science."
Source: Citation from Yale University, 1969, quoted by Shirley du Boulay, *Cicely Saunders*, 1984.

1918 Born Cicely Mary Strode Saunders, the first of three children. Their father was a property consultant.
1938 Starts at Oxford University, reading Politics, Philosophy and Economics.
1939 Leaves Oxford to train as a nurse but has to give up nursing because of back problems.
1944 Begins training as an almoner (medical social worker).
1945 Converts to Christianity.
1947 Starts work as almoner at St. Thomas' Hospital, London.
1948 Meets David Tasma and forms idea of starting a hospice. Starts voluntary work at St. Luke's Hospital for the dying.
1951 Begins training to become a doctor.
1957 Qualifies as a doctor.
1958 Starts research on care of the dying and works part-time at St. Joseph's Hospice.
1959 Draws up plans for St. Christopher's Hospice and starts raising money.
1967 Opening of St. Christopher's Hospice.
1960s onwards Lectures widely on the principles of hospice care.
1980 Marries Marian Bohusz-Szyszko. Is given honorary title "Dame of the British Empire."

Above, bereaved families meet for tea at St. Christopher's. The care which the hospice offers does not end with the death of the cancer patient. Relatives are encouraged to talk about their feelings, as a way of helping them come to terms with their loss, and many stay in touch with staff.

Conclusion

Marie Curie, Clara Barton and Cicely Saunders all showed that women have an important role in improving health conditions and in advancing scientific knowledge. They proved that women are as capable of understanding science as men. More than this, they can draw on their traditional caring skills and can ensure that new discoveries are applied in such a way as to bring better health as well as longer life.

In discovering radium, Marie Curie was pursuing scientific truth, and she also led the way to more effective treatment of cancer. Through her mobile X-ray service in World War I, she showed how important it is to diagnose an illness accurately before starting treatment.

Clara Barton campaigned for better conditions for soldiers injured in war and for more help to be given to victims of natural disasters such as fires, floods and earthquakes. Her relief effort was the forerunner of the many organizations which today speed emergency food and medical supplies all over the world.

Before Cicely Saunders started the modern hospice movement, thousands of dying patients lived in pain and fear. Today, her methods have spread far beyond the walls of St. Christopher's Hospice in London. Cancer is not limited to industrialized countries and doctors and nurses are carrying Cicely Saunders' message to hospices and hospitals on all continents.

All three of these women were single-minded in reaching their chosen goals. And as women in society, they experienced limitations and struggles. Each of the three women decided on their priorities. Marie Curie had little social life outside her work and family. Clara Barton remained single and Cicely Saunders did not marry until later in life.

More women now study the sciences than ever before. But many are still not encouraged to take these subjects at school. Medicine and science need young men and women to take up the challenge of today's health problems. Marie Curie, Clara Barton and Cicely Saunders all tackled the problems of their day. There will always be new targets awaiting future generations of scientists.

BOOKS TO READ

Marie Curie, Mollie Keller, Watts, 1987.
A detailed and thorough biography on the woman who revolutionized the world with her discovery of radium.

Marie Curie, Edwina Conner, Watts, 1987.
Geared toward a younger age group, full color illustrations and lively text recreate the eventful life of Marie Curie.

Radioactivity: From the Curies to the Atomic Age, Tom McGowen, Watts, 1986.
Covers early advances in physics emphasizing the work of the Curies and goes on to discuss the recent use of radioactivity — from treating cancer to the threat of the atomic bomb. Includes photos, diagrams, bibliography and index.

Women Pioneers of Science, rev. ed., by Louis Haber, published by Harcourt Brace Jovanovich, 1979.

Radiation, Mark Pettigrew, Watts, 1986.
Reader involvement is encouraged in this illustrated, full color volume. Light, heat, X-rays, radio waves and gamma rays are among the topics of radiation discussed here, along with explanations and ways of detecting and measuring radioactivity.

A Social History of Medicine,
F. F. Cartwright, Longman, 1977.
For the more advanced student. A guide to the social changes which have triggered advances in medicine.

The American Red Cross, written and edited by Patrick Gilbo, Harper & Row, 1981.
Largely pictorial history of the American Red Cross.

Compact History of the US Red Cross, Charles Hurd, Hawthorn, 1959.
Interesting and more detailed account of the development of the American Red Cross.

Clara Barton: Founder of the American Red Cross, Augusta Stevenson, Bobbs-Merrill, 1983.

Medicine: The Body and Healing, Gordon Jackson, Watts, 1984.
Full color illustrations, diagrams and an interesting text provide an excellent introduction to the structure and functions of the major systems of the human body. Also includes a close look at the main causes of illness, how the body fights infection, and discusses medicines currently used to combat various illnesses.

The Last Hundred Years: Medicine, Daniel Cohen, Ms. Evans & Co., 1981. Illus.

Medical Ethics, Carl Heintze, Watts, 1987.
Specific cases and examples are discussed regarding the dilemmas faced by doctors, patients and society in dealing with such important issues as organ transplants, euthanasia, and medical care for the poor.

Time chart

Nurses play a crucial part in health care. They are often the first to be aware of a change in a patient's condition. They are also an important source of information for patients who may still find doctors intimidating and hard to talk to. Today in Britain, the National Health Service is facing a crisis as funding is cut and wards are shut down in hospitals that are short of staff. Many nurses feel undervalued and are leaving the profession for better paid careers.

1800–1830s Europe and USA
Building programs for roads, sewage systems and fresh water supplies get under way as governments realize that epidemics are linked to poor sanitation and personal hygiene.

1860 England
Florence Nightingale establishes a training school for nurses at St. Thomas' Hospital, London. She had nursed soldiers in the Crimean War (1854–1856), where **Mary Seacole** had also worked with the wounded.

1860s France
Louis Pasteur shows that infections are transmitted by organisms in the enviroment. This opens the way for the practice of antisepsis in hospitals and the development of vaccines.

1861–1865 USA
The American Civil War makes the government aware of the results of bad diet and living conditions. Women, including **Clara Barton** and **Dorothea Dix**, demonstrate the need for relief organizations to help the wounded.

1882 USA
The American government follows the European example and sets up its own Red Cross to get food, medical supplies and other help to victims of war or natural disasters.

1890s France
The earlier discoveries in microbiology are followed by important developments in physics by the Polish physicist, **Marie Curie**, including the identification of radioactivity and the isolation of radium.

1914–1918 Europe
World War I demonstrates the importance of recent scientific discoveries, including antisepsis and X-rays. Relief agencies play an important role in getting food and medical supplies to the troops.

1940s England
The development of antibiotics reduces the annual death toll from infectious diseases such as tuberculosis.

1948 England
The National Health Service is set up to bring free health care to everyone, regardless of their ability to pay.

1960s England
Doctors begin to recognize the need for better care for the dying. **Cicely Saunders** pioneers the development of the modern hospice movement, with the setting up of St. Christopher's Hospice in London.

1970s–1980s Europe and USA
Growing realization that provision needs to be made for the chronically sick, the elderly and the mentally ill, as well as for those who can be cured by high-tech medicine.

Glossary

Antibiotic A drug, artificially made or produced by living organisms, which can kill or inhibit the growth of bacteria, but not other micro-organisms such as viruses.

Antisepsis The prevention of infection by destroying or inhibiting the growth of bacteria.

Bacteria Micro-organisms found throughout nature, responsible for infections such as typhoid, whooping cough and Legionnaires' disease.

Cancer Uncontrolled new growth of cells which is capable of spreading to or invading other parts of the body.

Element A substance which cannot be broken down by chemical means into simpler substances.

Epidemic A disease which attacks a large number of people at one time and spreads very rapidly.

Geneva Convention Agreement drawn up by the European leaders in 1864, governing the treatment of wounded soliders and prisoners of war.

Industrialization The extensive introduction of machinery to manufacturing that took place in the late 18th and early 19th centuries. Machines replaced people. Instead of working at home, many people went out to work in factories.

Magnetic resonance imaging A new technique for producing pictures of the internal organs and tissues of the body. Relies on signals produced by atoms in the body when it is placed in a strong magnetic field and radiowaves are beamed on to it.

Micro-organism A small microbe, such as bacterium or virus, which can only be seen under the microscope.

Morphine Powerful painkilling drug also capable of causing hallucinations if misused.

Ore A natural substance from which metal may be extracted.

Penicillin A substance produced by the mold *Penicillium*, which has anti-bacterial activity.

Radioactivity Powerful particles and rays produced by atoms with unstable nuclei.

Scientific revolution Period in the 17th and 18th centuries when a series of major advances in science and medicine were made. These included the establishment of the laws of physics, the nature of blood flow around the body, the detailed description of the anatomy of the body, and the development of medical diagnosis and surgical technique.

Sepsis Severe and potentially life-threatening infection.

Tumor Abnormal growth of cells which may or may not be cancerous.

Ultrasound A new technique for producing pictures of the internal organs and tissues of the body. It relies on "echoes" produced by soundwaves bounced off the surface of the body.

Urbanization The growth or development of towns, linked to people leaving the country for the towns.

Vaccination The use of small amounts of infectious agents to give immunity against diseases such as typhoid, whooping cough, polio.

Venereal disease Sexually transmitted disease.

Virus A tiny micro-organism, much smaller than bacteria, responsible for infections such as colds, flu, chickenpox and polio.

X-rays Powerful rays, invisible to the naked eye, produced by certain chemicals or electrically. They are used in diagnosis and in cancer treatment.

PLACES TO VISIT

The following organizations may be able to help with additional information. Write to them to ask what services they can offer, and whether it is possible to make an appointment to visit them:

FRANCE
Institut Pasteur,
25, Rue du Docteur Roux,
75724 Paris 15.

USA
American Red Cross,
17th and D Streets, NW
Washington, DC 20006.

ENGLAND
Wellcome Museum of the History of Medicine,
Science Museum,
Exhibition Road,
London SW7.

Index